IT'S A FACT!
3

IT'S A FACT!
3

Hamlyn Paperbacks

IT'S A FACT! 3

ISBN 0 600 20090 6

First published in Great Britain 1980
by Hamlyn Paperbacks
Copyright © 1980 by Kendal Fact Finders

Hamlyn Paperbacks are published by
The Hamlyn Publishing Group Ltd,
Astronaut House,
Feltham,
Middlesex, England

(Paperback Division: Hamlyn Paperbacks,
Banda House, Cambridge Grove,
Hammersmith, London W6 0LE)

Reproduced, printed and bound in Great Britain by
Cox & Wyman Ltd, Reading

The publishers have no reason to doubt the accuracy of
the material in this book but point out that in some cases
it is impossible to verify the information.

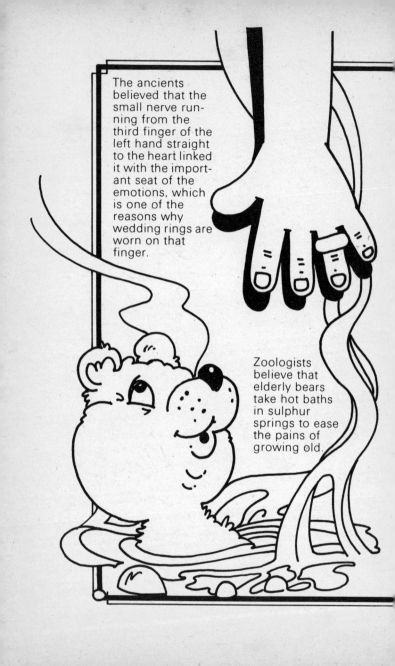

The ancients believed that the small nerve running from the third finger of the left hand straight to the heart linked it with the important seat of the emotions, which is one of the reasons why wedding rings are worn on that finger.

Zoologists believe that elderly bears take hot baths in sulphur springs to ease the pains of growing old.

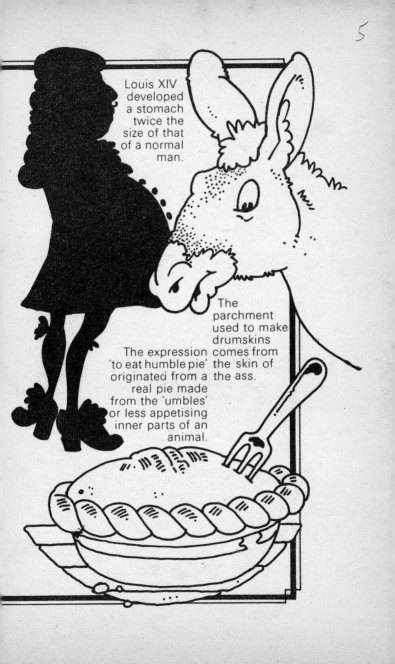

Louis XIV developed a stomach twice the size of that of a normal man.

The parchment used to make drumskins comes from the skin of the ass.

The expression 'to eat humble pie' originated from a real pie made from the 'umbles' or less appetising inner parts of an animal.

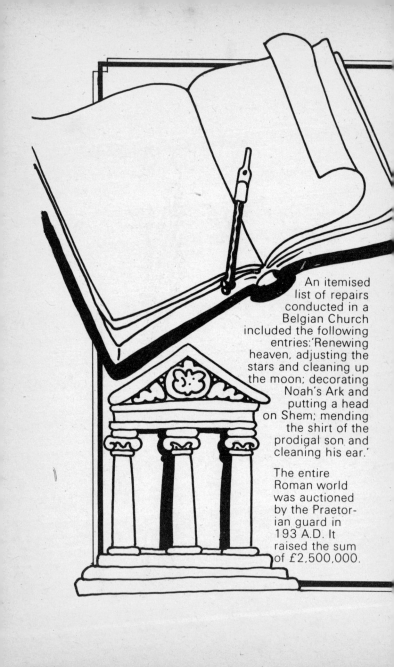

An itemised
list of repairs
conducted in a
Belgian Church
included the following
entries:'Renewing
heaven, adjusting the
stars and cleaning up
the moon; decorating
Noah's Ark and
putting a head
on Shem; mending
the shirt of the
prodigal son and
cleaning his ear.'

The entire
Roman world
was auctioned
by the Praetor-
ian guard in
193 A.D. It
raised the sum
of £2,500,000.

An apple was called a napple at one time.

Most people move about forty times in their sleep during the night. Insomniacs may move as many as seventy times.

All the ants that you see working frantically in ant-armies are female.

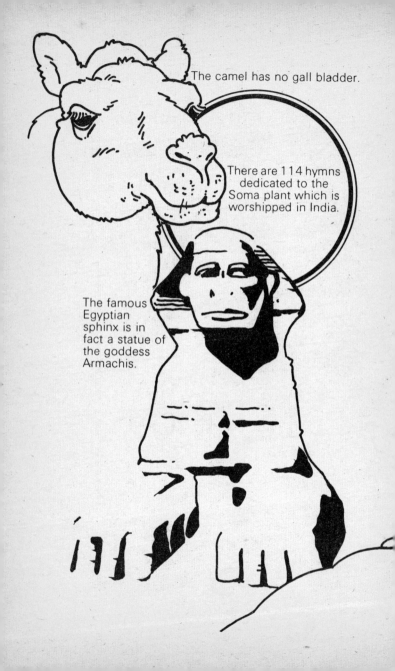

The camel has no gall bladder.

There are 114 hymns dedicated to the Soma plant which is worshipped in India.

The famous Egyptian sphinx is in fact a statue of the goddess Armachis.

In 1820 a man led his wife to the cattle market in Canterbury and sold her for five shillings (25p).

The first medical thermometers were so big and contained so much mercury that they needed five minutes to register the patient's temperature.

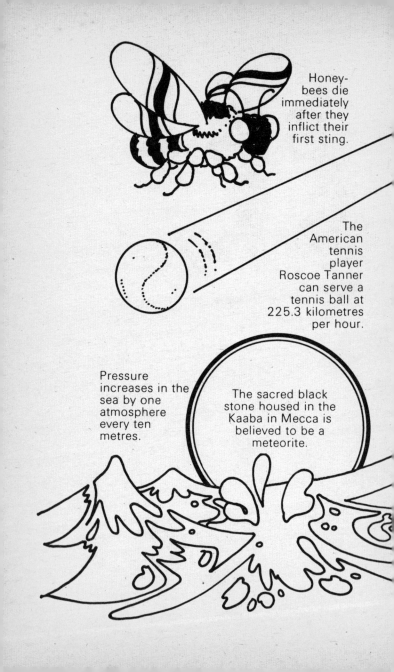

Honey-bees die immediately after they inflict their first sting.

The American tennis player Roscoe Tanner can serve a tennis ball at 225.3 kilometres per hour.

Pressure increases in the sea by one atmosphere every ten metres.

The sacred black stone housed in the Kaaba in Mecca is believed to be a meteorite.

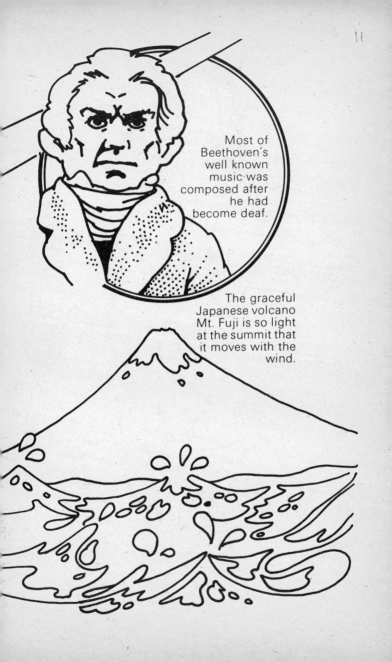

Most of Beethoven's well known music was composed after he had become deaf.

The graceful Japanese volcano Mt. Fuji is so light at the summit that it moves with the wind.

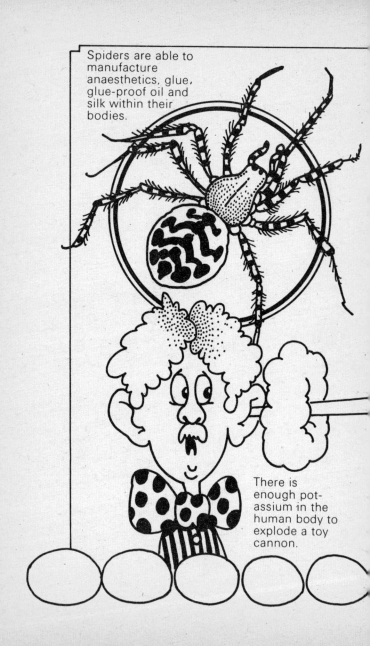

Spiders are able to manufacture anaesthetics, glue, glue-proof oil and silk within their bodies.

There is enough potassium in the human body to explode a toy cannon.

The sixteenth century French astrologer Nostradamus predicted the French Revolution, the rise of Fascist leaders like Hitler and Mussolini and the destruction of cities from the air.

The sphinx was carved from one piece of stone.

Every tenth egg is larger than the preceding nine.

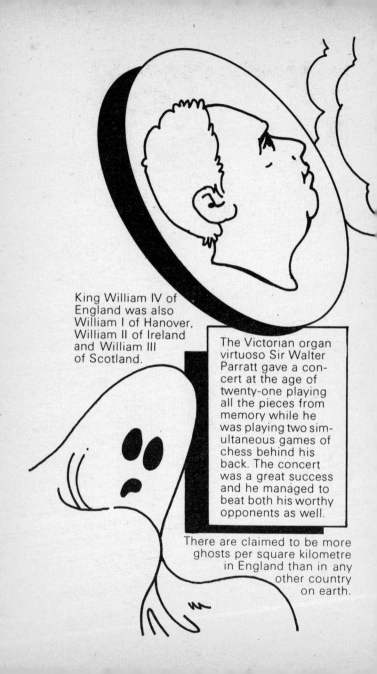

King William IV of England was also William I of Hanover, William II of Ireland and William III of Scotland.

The Victorian organ virtuoso Sir Walter Parratt gave a concert at the age of twenty-one playing all the pieces from memory while he was playing two simultaneous games of chess behind his back. The concert was a great success and he managed to beat both his worthy opponents as well.

There are claimed to be more ghosts per square kilometre in England than in any other country on earth.

Soya beans are used in the manufacture of glue, paint, plastics and explosives.

On her second voyage to the New World the 'Mayflower' carried a cargo of slaves.

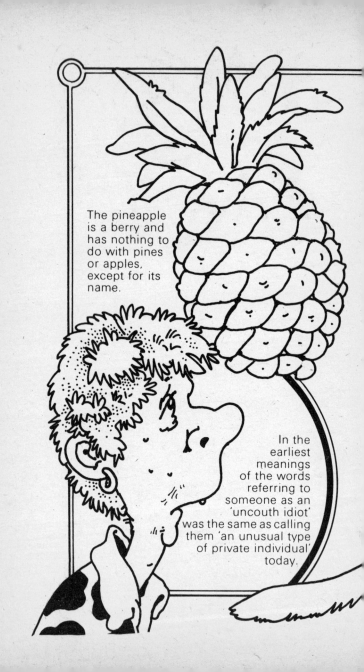

The pineapple is a berry and has nothing to do with pines or apples, except for its name.

In the earliest meanings of the words referring to someone as an 'uncouth idiot' was the same as calling them 'an unusual type of private individual' today.

Unlike imitation diamonds the real ones always feel cold.

Any whole number decreased by the sum of its digits will leave a remainder that can be divided by 9.

The Median prophet Zoroaster who founded the ancient fire-worshipping religion of Persia lived on nothing but cheese for thirty years.

It is possible for ferrets to catch colds in the same way that we do.

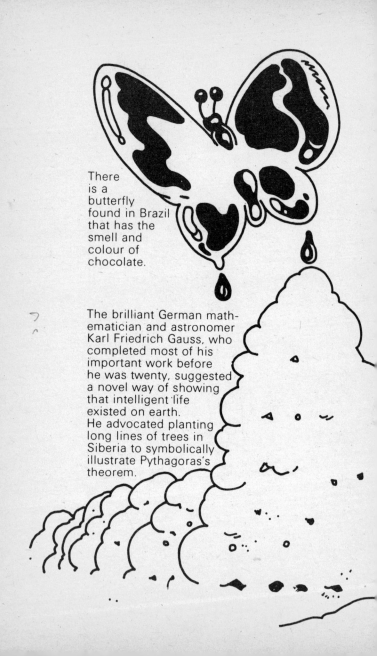

There
is a
butterfly
found in Brazil
that has the
smell and
colour of
chocolate.

The brilliant German mathematician and astronomer
Karl Friedrich Gauss, who
completed most of his
important work before
he was twenty, suggested
a novel way of showing
that intelligent life
existed on earth.
He advocated planting
long lines of trees in
Siberia to symbolically
illustrate Pythagoras's
theorem.

British barristers still wear black in mourning for the wife of William III, even though Queen Mary died in 1694.

There are at least eighty different varieties of rice grown in India.

An eccentric French heiress Madame de la Bresse left her fortune to be spent on buying clothes for snowmen.

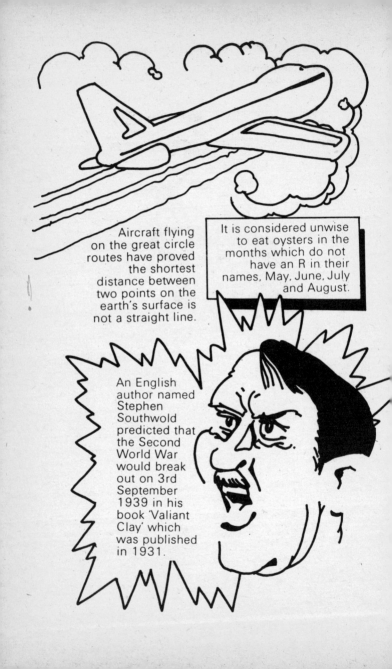

Aircraft flying on the great circle routes have proved the shortest distance between two points on the earth's surface is not a straight line.

It is considered unwise to eat oysters in the months which do not have an R in their names, May, June, July and August.

An English author named Stephen Southwold predicted that the Second World War would break out on 3rd September 1939 in his book 'Valiant Clay' which was published in 1931.

The French Empress Marie Louise, who married Napoleon after he had divorced Josephine, possessed the remarkable ability of moving her ears at will and even turning them inside out.

In 1696 a tiny two-storey church was built inside a massive oak tree in Allouville, France.

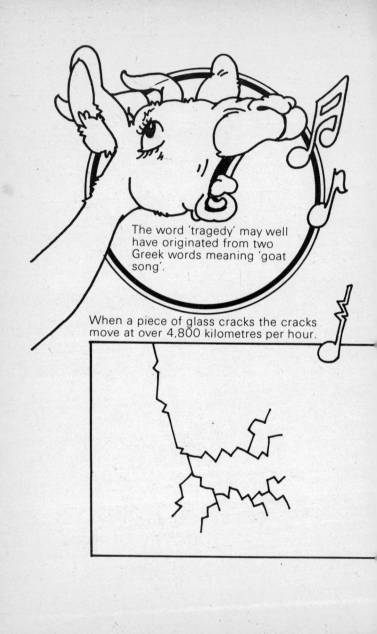

The word 'tragedy' may well have originated from two Greek words meaning 'goat song'.

When a piece of glass cracks the cracks move at over 4,800 kilometres per hour.

The super-
stitions
surrounding
the number 13
originate from
the Last
Supper, when
13 sat down
to eat.

Mercury, platinum,
tungsten and
uranium are all
heavier than gold.

Every night a
barn owl will
eat more
than its own
weight in
food. It later
disposes of
the pieces it
can't man-
age to eat.

Left-handed playing cards have pips in all four corners. Normal playing cards have pips in the top left-hand corner only.

The Empire State Building in New York City was built to be able to withstand a sway of 30 cm. from the perpendicular.

Lord Byron's boxing instructor, Gentleman Jackson, could sign his name with a 36 kilogramme weight balanced on his arm at the same time.

The lunar year has 354 days, the common year has 365 days and the Julian year has 365¹/₄ days.

A yak has the skeleton of a bison, the hair of a goat, the tail of a horse, the head of a cow and makes a grunt like a pig.

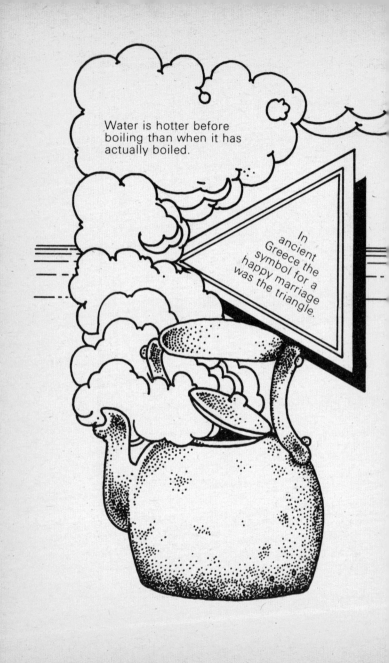

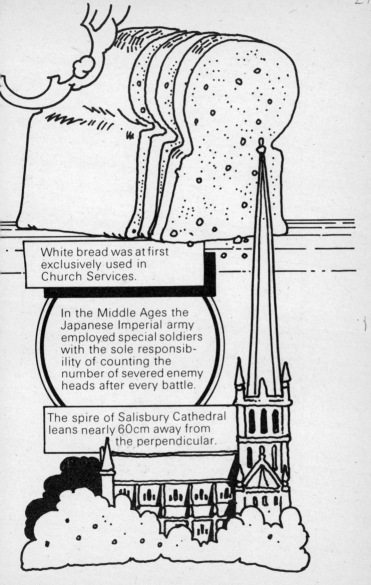

White bread was at first exclusively used in Church Services.

In the Middle Ages the Japanese Imperial army employed special soldiers with the sole responsibility of counting the number of severed enemy heads after every battle.

The spire of Salisbury Cathedral leans nearly 60cm away from the perpendicular.

The seventeenth king of
Poland, John III, was born,
crowned and married on
the same day of the same
month, June 17.
Ironically he died on
June 17 as well.

The original
Cinderella was
Egyptian.

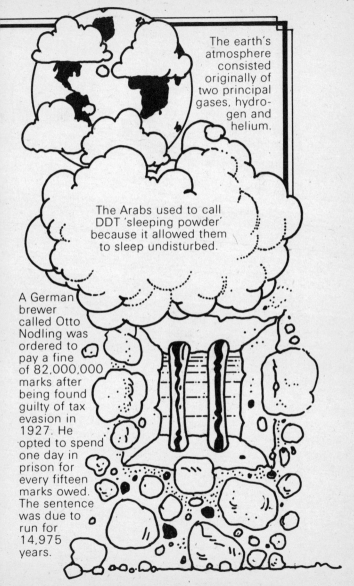

The earth's atmosphere consisted originally of two principal gases, hydrogen and helium.

The Arabs used to call DDT 'sleeping powder' because it allowed them to sleep undisturbed.

A German brewer called Otto Nodling was ordered to pay a fine of 82,000,000 marks after being found guilty of tax evasion in 1927. He opted to spend one day in prison for every fifteen marks owed. The sentence was due to run for 14,975 years.

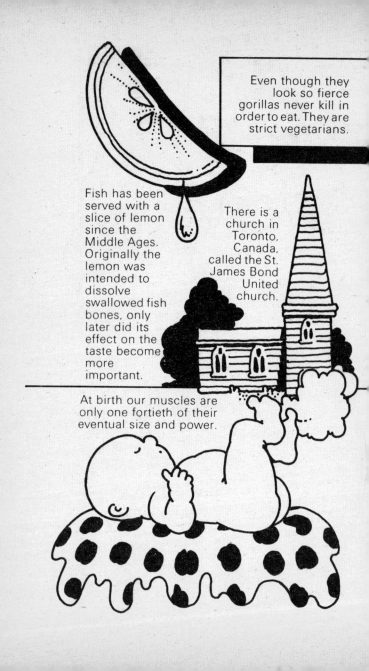

Even though they look so fierce gorillas never kill in order to eat. They are strict vegetarians.

Fish has been served with a slice of lemon since the Middle Ages. Originally the lemon was intended to dissolve swallowed fish bones, only later did its effect on the taste become more important.

There is a church in Toronto, Canada, called the St. James Bond United church.

At birth our muscles are only one fortieth of their eventual size and power.

The foot-and-mouth epidemic in Britain of 1967-68 cost an estimated £150,000,000.

The smallest colony in the world is the Pacific Island of Pitcairn which has a population of under one hundred, who are principally Seventh Day Adventists.

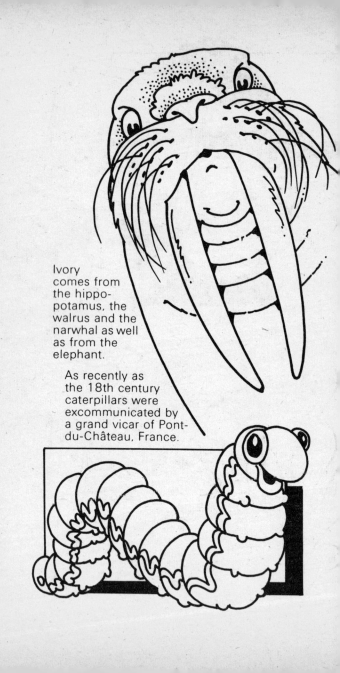

Ivory comes from the hippopotamus, the walrus and the narwhal as well as from the elephant.

As recently as the 18th century caterpillars were excommunicated by a grand vicar of Pont-du-Château, France.

Birds are sometimes able to set their own broken wings.

The inventor of the compass, a Chinese called Chou Kung, had a hand which could swivel in a complete circle on the end of his wrist.

There is a waterfall near Honolulu which 'falls' upwards.

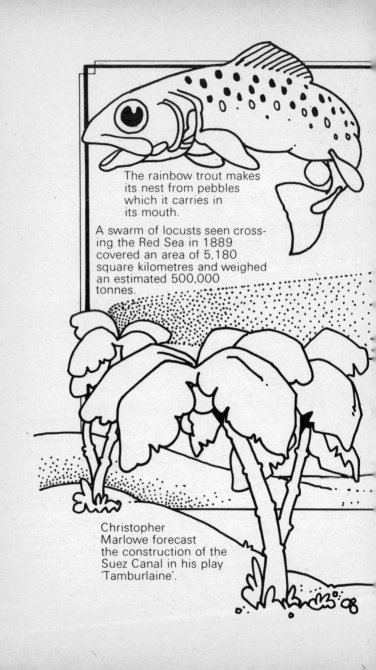

The rainbow trout makes
its nest from pebbles
which it carries in
its mouth.

A swarm of locusts seen cross-
ing the Red Sea in 1889
covered an area of 5,180
square kilometres and weighed
an estimated 500,000
tonnes.

Christopher
Marlowe forecast
the construction of the
Suez Canal in his play
'Tamburlaine'.

Queen Elizabeth I was the only British Sovereign between William I and Elizabeth II who did not effectively possess any land outside England and Wales.

? India etc.

In the state of Minnesota it is against the law to hang male and female underwear on the same washing-line.

A ship is between four and six times more efficient in converting energy into work than a duck.

80 per cent of the population of India live in communities of less than 5,000 inhabitants.

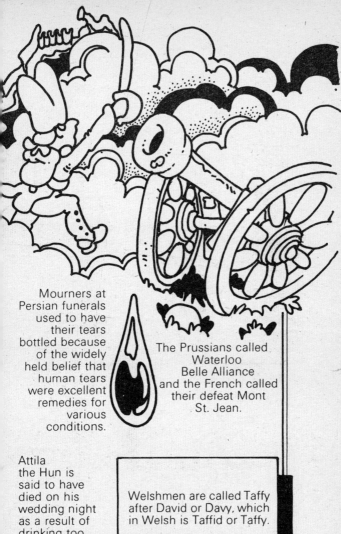

Mourners at Persian funerals used to have their tears bottled because of the widely held belief that human tears were excellent remedies for various conditions.

The Prussians called Waterloo Belle Alliance and the French called their defeat Mont St. Jean.

Attila the Hun is said to have died on his wedding night as a result of drinking too much mead.

Welshmen are called Taffy after David or Davy, which in Welsh is Taffid or Taffy.

With the exception of Antarctica all the continents are wider in the north than in the south.

The vapour trail from a comet with a mass of 250,070 cubic kilometres would weigh as much as the air you inhale in one breath.

37 cannot be divided by any other number but it will divide 111,222,333,444,555 etc. to 999.

During the siege of Delhi in 1296, the Moslem invader Ala-ud-Din was forced to use bags of gold as ammunition for his artillery.

The Chinese used to believe that eclipses were caused by the appetite of a hungry dragon.

The first gold brought back by Columbus was used to gild the ceiling of the church of Santa Maria Maggiore.

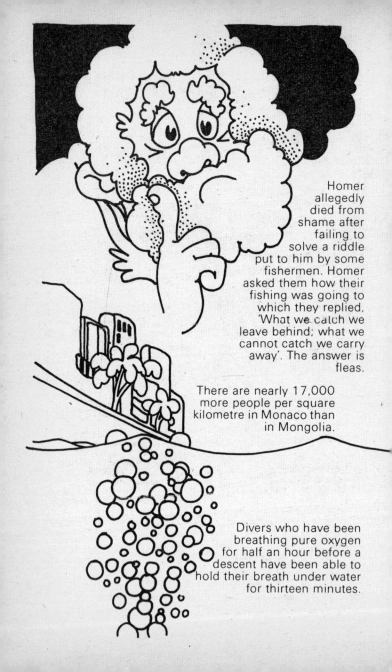

Homer allegedly died from shame after failing to solve a riddle put to him by some fishermen. Homer asked them how their fishing was going to which they replied, 'What we catch we leave behind; what we cannot catch we carry away'. The answer is fleas.

There are nearly 17,000 more people per square kilometre in Monaco than in Mongolia.

Divers who have been breathing pure oxygen for half an hour before a descent have been able to hold their breath under water for thirteen minutes.

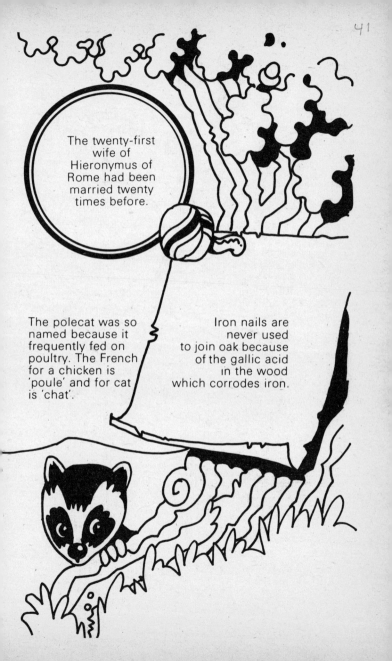

The twenty-first
wife of
Hieronymus of
Rome had been
married twenty
times before.

The polecat was so
named because it
frequently fed on
poultry. The French
for a chicken is
'poule' and for cat
is 'chat'.

Iron nails are
never used
to join oak because
of the gallic acid
in the wood
which corrodes iron.

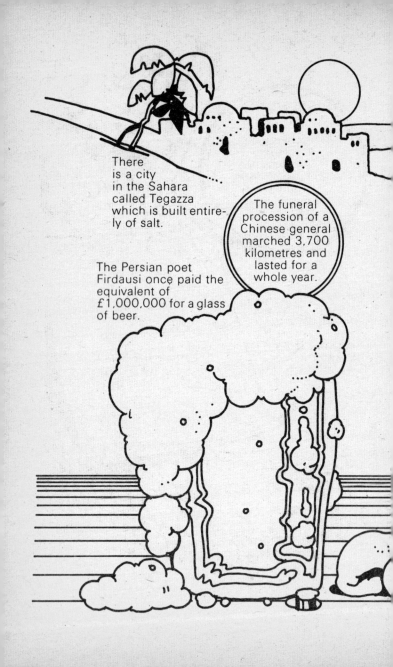

There is a city in the Sahara called Tegazza which is built entirely of salt.

The funeral procession of a Chinese general marched 3,700 kilometres and lasted for a whole year.

The Persian poet Firdausi once paid the equivalent of £1,000,000 for a glass of beer.

OBLIGE

There is no word in English that rhymes with 'oblige'.

Seven normal sized men could fit inside the coat of Brobdingnagian Bright.

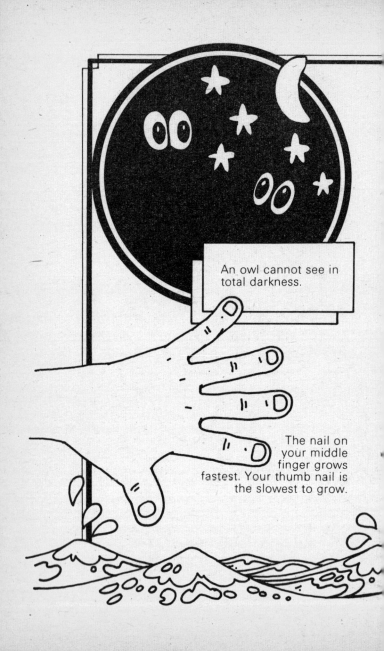

An owl cannot see in total darkness.

The nail on your middle finger grows fastest. Your thumb nail is the slowest to grow.

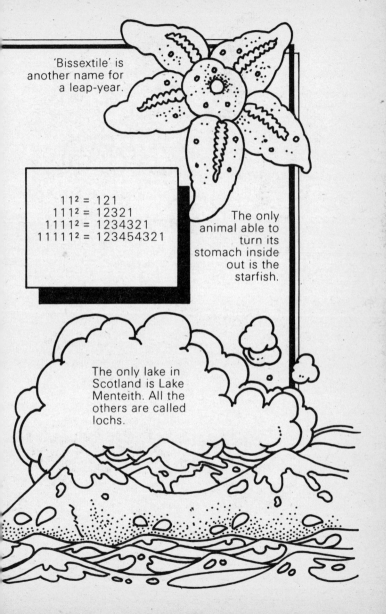

'Bissextile' is another name for a leap-year.

$11^2 = 121$
$111^2 = 12321$
$1111^2 = 1234321$
$11111^2 = 123454321$

The only animal able to turn its stomach inside out is the starfish.

The only lake in Scotland is Lake Menteith. All the others are called lochs.

A queen bee only leaves her hive to lead out a swarm and to go on her wedding flight.

One of the moons of Mars called Deimos rises and sets twice a day.

The Jeep got its name from its original initials G.P., which stood for General Purpose vehicle.

The bells that are tolled at funerals and the shots that are fired at military burials are Christian adaptations of pagan practices of frightening away evil spirits.

François I, King of France, banned the wearing of whiskers on pain of death.

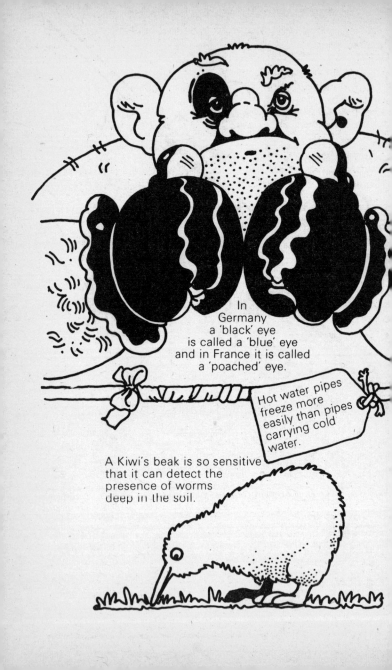

In Germany a 'black' eye is called a 'blue' eye and in France it is called a 'poached' eye.

Hot water pipes freeze more easily than pipes carrying cold water.

A Kiwi's beak is so sensitive that it can detect the presence of worms deep in the soil.

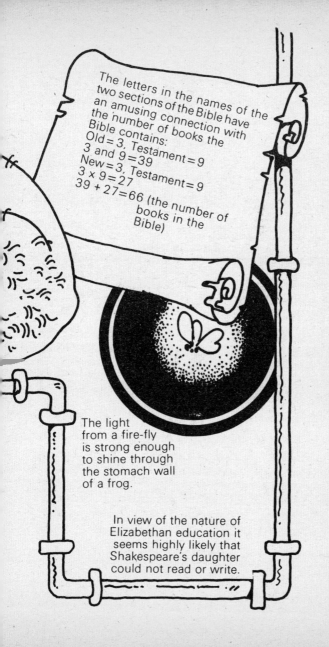

The letters in the names of the two sections of the Bible have an amusing connection with the number of books the Bible contains:

Old = 3, Testament = 9

3 and 9 = 39

New = 3, Testament = 9

3 × 9 = 27

39 + 27 = 66 (the number of books in the Bible)

The light from a fire-fly is strong enough to shine through the stomach wall of a frog.

In view of the nature of Elizabethan education it seems highly likely that Shakespeare's daughter could not read or write.

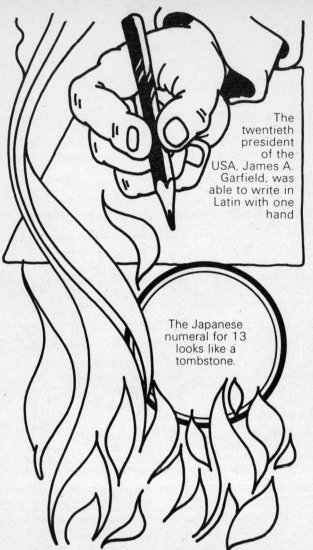

The twentieth president of the USA, James A. Garfield, was able to write in Latin with one hand

The Japanese numeral for 13 looks like a tombstone.

Wire wool burns faster than wool from the sheep's back.

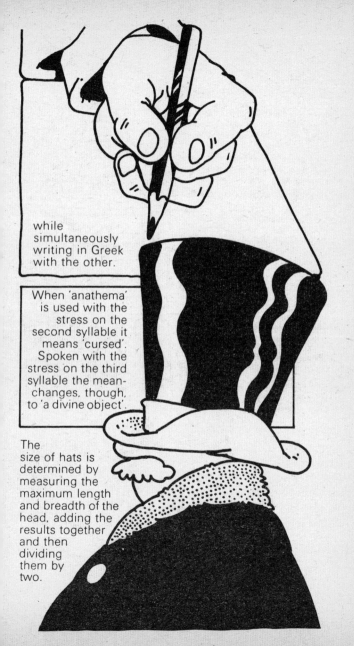

while
simultaneously
writing in Greek
with the other.

When 'anathema'
is used with the
stress on the
second syllable it
means 'cursed'.
Spoken with the
stress on the third
syllable the mean-
changes, though,
to 'a divine object'.

The
size of hats is
determined by
measuring the
maximum length
and breadth of the
head, adding the
results together
and then
dividing
them by
two.

51

The longest one word palindrome in English is 'redivider', which spells the same word reading the letters either forwards or backwards.

There is a speaking well in the village of Troo, Montoire, France, which repeats whole phrases spoken into it.

Sea otters have not one, but two coats of fur.

The 'chadouf' or water-raising song has been sung along the banks of the Nile for about 5,000 years.

One of the Moorish Kings of Spain, Abbad el Motaddid of Seville, used the skulls of enemies he had personally killed as flower pots.

On average more snow falls in the State of Virginia, in the eastern part of the USA, than in the Arctic lowlands.

Cockroaches have remained un-changed on earth for about 250,000,000 years.

Emperor Hirohito of Japan is an authority on the study of fish.

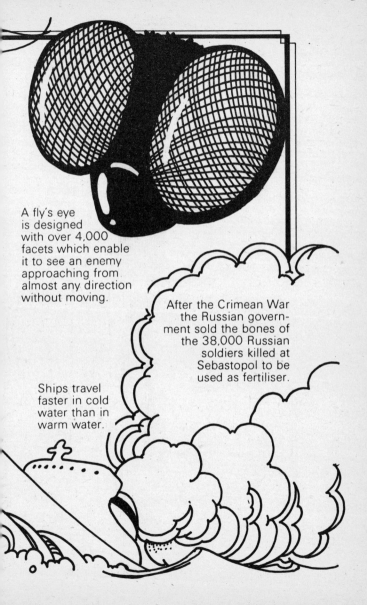

A fly's eye is designed with over 4,000 facets which enable it to see an enemy approaching from almost any direction without moving.

After the Crimean War the Russian government sold the bones of the 38,000 Russian soldiers killed at Sebastopol to be used as fertiliser.

Ships travel faster in cold water than in warm water.

The Sequeru cactus grows
branches that are sixteen
times taller than a man.

The so-called Prairie
dog is a rodent.

Although the
frigate bird
lives on fish it is
unable to swim
or land on the
water.

0.45 kilogrammes of
uranium contains
10,000,000,000,000,
000,000,000,000, explos-
ive neutrons which are
released in one millionth
of a second.

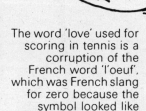

The word 'love' used for
scoring in tennis is a
corruption of the
French word 'l'oeuf',
which was French slang
for zero because the
symbol looked like
an egg.

The Vinegar
river, in Columbia,
contains so much
sulphuric acid and
hydrochloric acid that
it is so sour that no
fish can live in it.

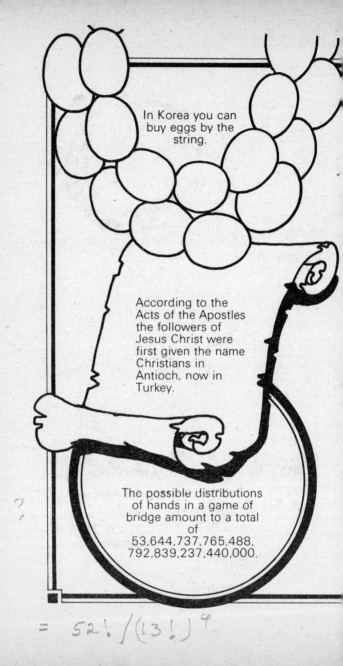

In Korea you can buy eggs by the string.

According to the Acts of the Apostles the followers of Jesus Christ were first given the name Christians in Antioch, now in Turkey.

The possible distributions of hands in a game of bridge amount to a total of 53,644,737,765,488,792,839,237,440,000.

= 52! / (13!)⁴

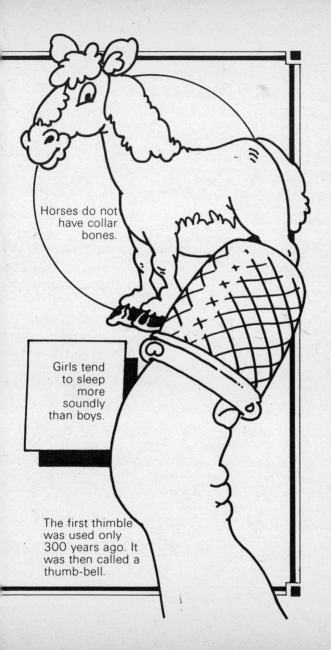

Horses do not have collar bones.

Girls tend to sleep more soundly than boys.

The first thimble was used only 300 years ago. It was then called a thumb-bell.

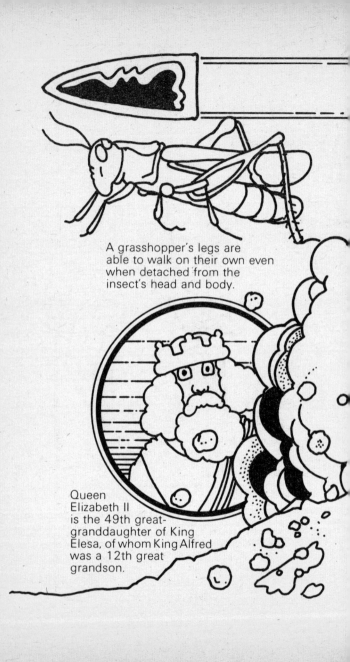

A grasshopper's legs are able to walk on their own even when detached from the insect's head and body.

Queen Elizabeth II is the 49th great-granddaughter of King Elesa, of whom King Alfred was a 12th great grandson.

The speed at which the earth revolves around the sun is roughly eight times faster than that at which a bullet leaves a gun.

A human hair laid on a bar of steel and then passed through a cold rolling mill would leave an imprint on the face of the steel.

A fortnight after the English opera singer Elizabeth Billington gave a stunning performance in Naples in 1794 she was blamed by the Neapolitans for causing an eruption of Vesuvius.

Some lichen are able to absorb half their own weight in water in ten minutes.

A Parisian music teacher, Alphonse Durand, christened seven of his children Do, Re Mi, Fa, Sol, La and Si. The eighth child was named Octave.

When you toasted a lady's health in ancient Rome it was customary to drink one glass for every letter of her name.

For several years Aurélien School published a rubber newspaper for the benefit of those who enjoyed reading it in their baths.

The shapes of letters O, B, P and F
reflect the shape of the mouth
when the sounds are made.
O indicates an open mouth,
B is the profile of sealed lips
pronouncing it. P shows the
lips partly open and
F is the P shape but
with the air escaping
to make the F
sound.

In 1910 there was an outbreak of the
plague in Sussex.

The English army's description of home as 'blighty' is derived from the Hindi word for a 'village', 'belayti'.

The skunk cabbage gets its name from the smell of rotting flesh that it exudes.

Monarch butterflies migrate more than 3,000 kilometres every year.

The actor Danny Kaye made his stage debut in the part of a watermelon seed.

The Etruscans were the first to use the eagle as a symbol of royal power.

Six locomotives were needed to pull a freight train that was nearly six kilometres long and that weighed almost forty-two thousand tonnes.

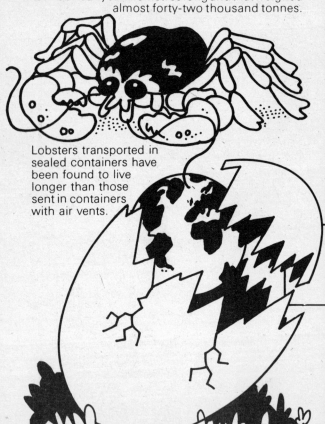

Lobsters transported in sealed containers have been found to live longer than those sent in containers with air vents.

The rings round Saturn are about 80,500 kilometres in circumference but only about 30 centimetres thick.

The ancient Egyptians believed that the world was hatched from an egg laid by the sacred ibis.

French artist Anne-Louis Girodet only painted at night by the light of forty candles stuck in the brim of his hat. He based his fees on the number of candles burned in the painting of every picture.

It takes a cicada 17 years to develop as a larva, but its adult life only lasts four weeks.

A Chamois can stand on an area not much larger than a 50p piece.

In Madagascar the silk from spiders' webs is woven into a cloth.

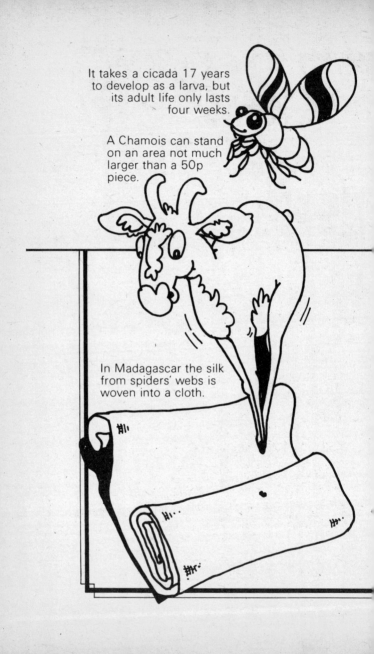

The fear of beds is known as 'clinophobia'.

Frau Sophie Bunnen, wife of a Prussian farmer, was reported to have given birth to eleven children in sixteen months. She produced sextuplets and quintuplets.

There is one acupuncture point in your body for each of the following conditions: boils, alcoholism and nymphomania.

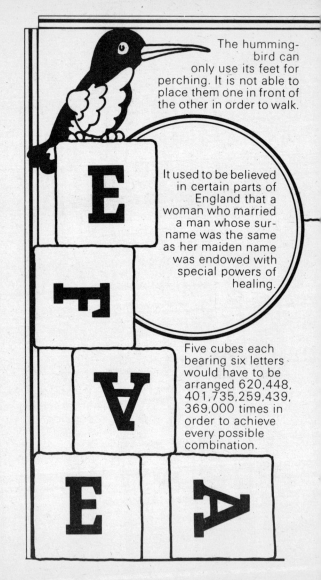

The humming-bird can only use its feet for perching. It is not able to place them one in front of the other in order to walk.

It used to be believed in certain parts of England that a woman who married a man whose surname was the same as her maiden name was endowed with special powers of healing.

Five cubes each bearing six letters would have to be arranged 620,448,401,735,259,439,369,000 times in order to achieve every possible combination.

6204484017352594393 69000
2 * 2 * 2 * 5 * 5 * 5 *
ADLEMAN Test for 6204484017352594393 69
Power Check 4 3 2
EC METHOD with limit ($B1=$ 2833 $B2=$ 1113320)
Curve 1
ADLEMAN Test for 10501475893
ADLEMAN Test for 5908 2019333

6204484017352594393 69000 =
2 * 2 * 2 * 5 * 5 * 5 * 10501475893 * 5908 2019333

5! 24 5 = 955514880

5! 65 = 933,120

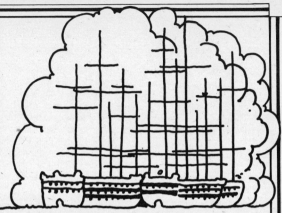

In January 1795 the entire Dutch fleet was captured by the French cavalry that crossed the frozen Zuider Zee to surround the beleaguered ships.

Moths cannot eat because they have neither mouths nor stomachs.

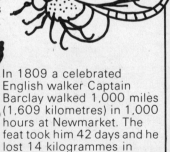

In 1809 a celebrated English walker Captain Barclay walked 1,000 miles (1,609 kilometres) in 1,000 hours at Newmarket. The feat took him 42 days and he lost 14 kilogrammes in weight.

The only naturally blue food is the Irish Bilberry.

All those wishing to be elected to official positions in ancient Rome used to wear white togas before the elections took place. The Latin word for 'white', 'candidus', gives us our word 'candidate'.

The Boya bird which is found in the Philippines weaves fireflies into its nest causing it to glow in the dark.

Johann Georg Krünitz wrote an encyclopaedia containing 242 volumes entirely in longhand.

A pythoness is a witch, not a female snake as might be expected.

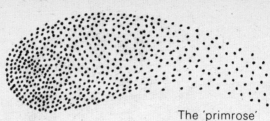

A medium sized swarm of locusts contains about one million insects and consumes about twenty tonnes of food a day.

The 'primrose' has nothing to do with roses. It is named after the French phrase 'primes rolles' meaning 'earliest little flowers'. The Old French word 'primerose' was the name given to what we now call a 'hollyhock'.

Military bugle calls were introduced into all sections of the army in the middle of the eighteenth century. The first publication of bugle calls appeared in 1798 and it is possible that some of these were composed by Emperor Franz Joseph who happened to be in Britain at the time.

The question mark ? developed from the early practice of putting the first and last letters of the word 'questio' after a sentence. As this practice increased the 'q' was written above the 'o', until finally the 'q' degenerated into ? and the 'o' became simply . .

The first person reported to have committed suicide by falling onto his own sword was King Saul.

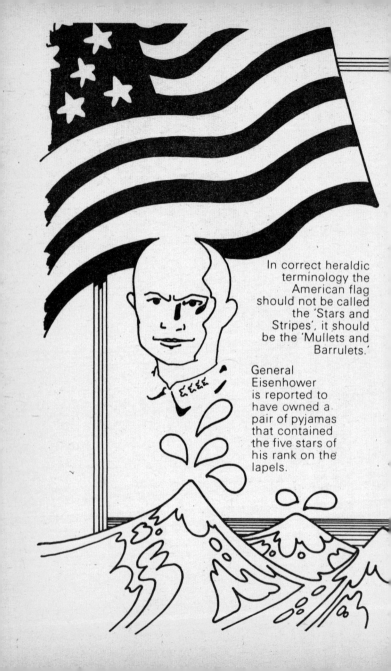

In correct heraldic terminology the American flag should not be called the 'Stars and Stripes', it should be the 'Mullets and Barrulets.'

General Eisenhower is reported to have owned a pair of pyjamas that contained the five stars of his rank on the lapels.

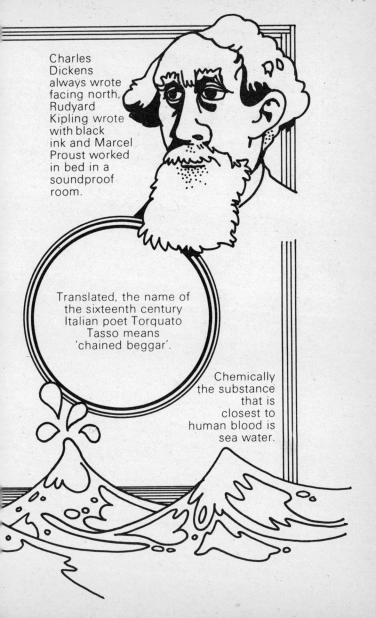

Charles Dickens always wrote facing north, Rudyard Kipling wrote with black ink and Marcel Proust worked in bed in a soundproof room.

Translated, the name of the sixteenth century Italian poet Torquato Tasso means 'chained beggar'.

Chemically the substance that is closest to human blood is sea water.

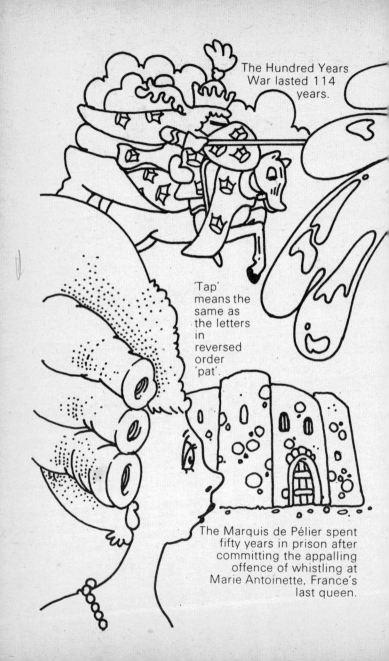

The Hundred Years War lasted 114 years.

'Tap' means the same as the letters in reversed order 'pat'.

The Marquis de Pélier spent fifty years in prison after committing the appalling offence of whistling at Marie Antoinette, France's last queen.

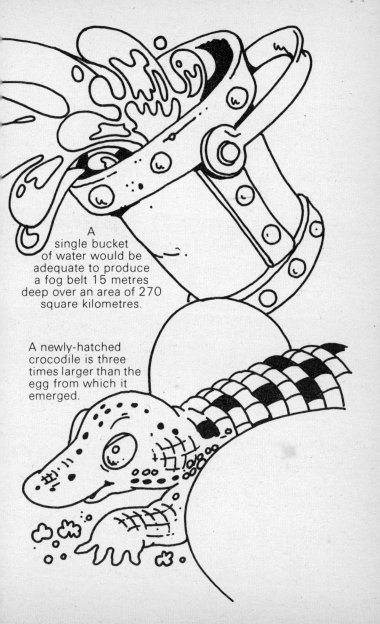

A
single bucket
of water would be
adequate to produce
a fog belt 15 metres
deep over an area of 270
square kilometres.

A newly-hatched
crocodile is three
times larger than the
egg from which it
emerged.

There are references in the Talmud, the canon of Jewish law, to oral contraceptives and artificial insemination.

The oldest moon rock so far brought back to earth was found to contain twenty times more uranium, thorium and potassium than any moon rock that had been previously studied.

The Hurricane-plant is protected from being destroyed by high winds by the holes in its leaves.

Luminous bacteria, that have the ability to give off light, have been cooled to a temperature of −190°C and found to be alive when they were warmed up.

In Jamaica there are some oysters that live in trees.

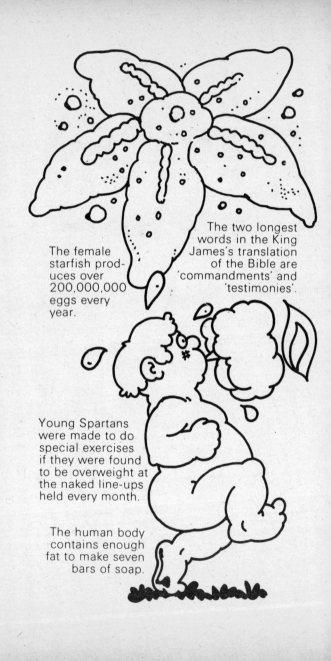

The female starfish produces over 200,000,000 eggs every year.

The two longest words in the King James's translation of the Bible are 'commandments' and 'testimonies'.

Young Spartans were made to do special exercises if they were found to be overweight at the naked line-ups held every month.

The human body contains enough fat to make seven bars of soap.

The Belgian hare is a rabbit.

Petrol and paraffin extinguish fires in bales of cotton more efficiently than water.

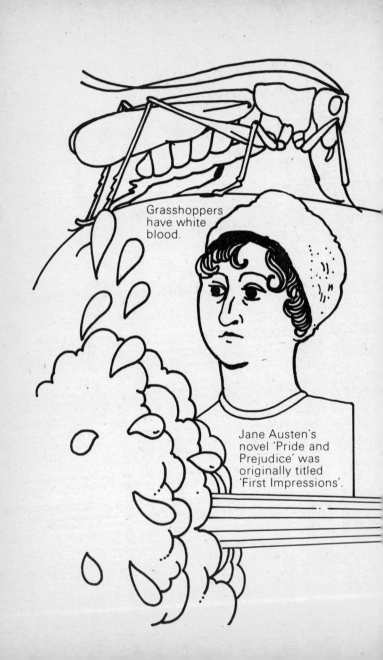

Grasshoppers have white blood.

Jane Austen's novel 'Pride and Prejudice' was originally titled 'First Impressions'.

If you
wanted
to break off
your engagement
in medieval
England you sent
your betrothed a
sprig of lilac.

Christian Heinrich of Lübeck
was able to talk when he was
eight weeks old and he knew
pieces from the Pentateuch
and the Bible at the age of
thirteen months.

The water-jets that are used in the
manufacture of high carbon steel
are strong enough to blast a hole
through a pine plank.

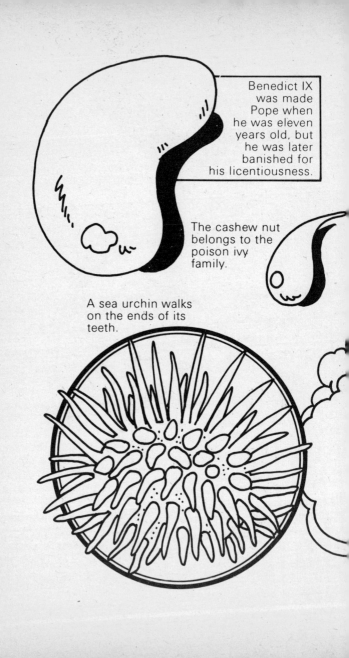

Benedict IX was made Pope when he was eleven years old, but he was later banished for his licentiousness.

The cashew nut belongs to the poison ivy family.

A sea urchin walks on the ends of its teeth.

A brush used for applying varnish gives 100 times as much wear as one used for putting on paint.

The first and last letters of all the continents' names are alike.

One of the earliest-designed airships resembled a canoe with paddles that was held aloft by several glass balloons.

It is impossible to see a gaggle of geese flying. In the air a formation of geese is called a skein.

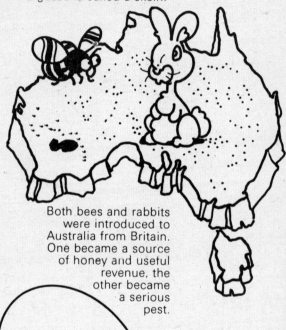

Both bees and rabbits were introduced to Australia from Britain. One became a source of honey and useful revenue, the other became a serious pest.

If you shake an egg enough it is possible to make it stand on end. The yolk breaks and sinks to the bottom of the shell.

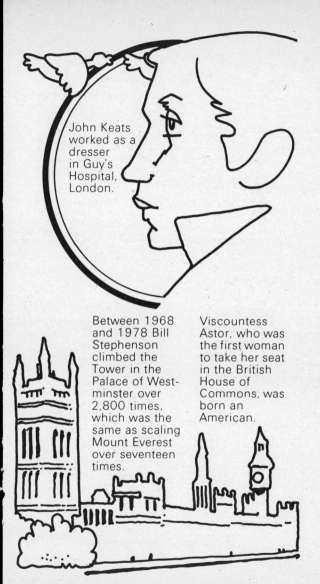

John Keats worked as a dresser in Guy's Hospital, London.

Between 1968 and 1978 Bill Stephenson climbed the Tower in the Palace of Westminster over 2,800 times, which was the same as scaling Mount Everest over seventeen times.

Viscountess Astor, who was the first woman to take her seat in the British House of Commons, was born an American.

The collective noun for barrage
balloon is balloon barrage.

'Tea' used to be pronounced 'tay' in the late seventeenth century.

The first sun-heated steam engine was built in 1864, though solar energy had been used to power toys as early as 1615.

Pope Paul IV was so horrified by the naked figures painted by Michelangelo in the 'Last Judgement' that he commissioned another artist, Daniele de Volterra, to 'clothe' them.

Madame de Pompadour was the first person to own a pet goldfish in France.

The presence of blue blood indicates one of the following conditions: that you are being asphyxiated or you are a lobster.

The Oscars awarded by the American Academy of Motion Picture Arts and Sciences during the Second World War were made out of wood to conserve metal.

Surveys conducted
among academics
have shown that
professors who smoke
are twice as likely to
write books as those
who do not.

The
Great White
Shark is the only
creature living in the sea
that has no natural enemies –
even killer whales avoid it.

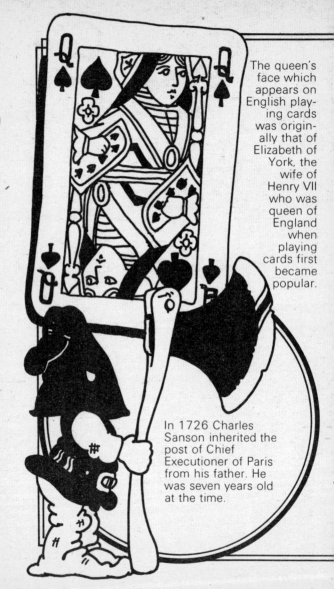

c1500 ?

The queen's face which appears on English playing cards was originally that of Elizabeth of York, the wife of Henry VII who was queen of England when playing cards first became popular.

In 1726 Charles Sanson inherited the post of Chief Executioner of Paris from his father. He was seven years old at the time.

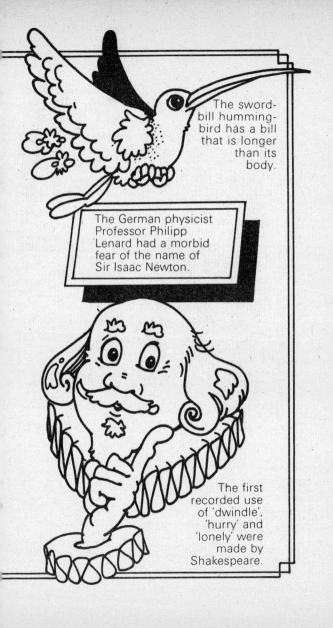

The sword-bill humming-bird has a bill that is longer than its body.

The German physicist Professor Philipp Lenard had a morbid fear of the name of Sir Isaac Newton.

The first recorded use of 'dwindle', 'hurry' and 'lonely' were made by Shakespeare.

Benjamin Franklin was the youngest son of a youngest son of a youngest son of a youngest son.

A Neapolitan citizen called Giuseppe de Mai was born with two hearts.

A famous Norwegian cross-country runner Mensen Ernst ran from Paris to Moscow in a fortnight. Swimming 13 large rivers he still managed to average 200 kilometres a day.

If it was possible for
the human voice to
be carried naturally
for great distances
through the air, it
would take fourteen
hours for a shout
bellowed in
Australia to
be heard on
the west coast of
the USA.

At an altitude of 7,620
metres a pilot can see for
a distance of 312
kilometres.

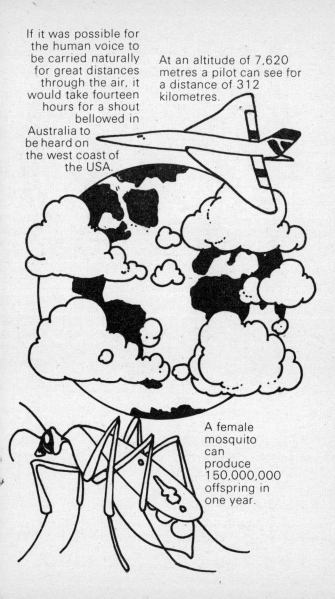

A female
mosquito
can
produce
150,000,000
offspring in
one year.

The Portuguese prince, Henry the Navigator, had never navigated a ship in his life and indeed had never left Portugal when he was given the title.

The backbone of a camel is perfectly straight.

Adrienne Cuyot of Belgium was engaged 652 times and married 53 times over a period of 23 years.

According to his contemporaries, Sir Isaac Newton may have been a mathematician of genius, but he was quite incapable of performing any simple mental arithmatic.

Haj Ahmel, who was once Bey of Algeria, had 385 wives who all came from different parts of the world so that none of them could communicate.

A wealthy Austrian widow, Frau Mathilde Kovacs, took revenge on her relatives, who failed to show proper regard for her pet cat, by burning her entire fortune before she died.

It used to be believed that advice given on the treatment of whooping cough would prove to be successful if the person giving it was riding a piebald horse.

The enormous Sahuaro cactus which grows in the south-west of the USA and in Mexico is known to be able to survive for three years without water.

Erasmus stated
that any man who
failed to catch syphilis
was, in his opinion,
'ignobilis et rusticans',
a base oaf.

Since a frog has no neck it
is neither able to turn its head
nor bend it towards the
ground.

The earliest pictures of Father Christmas, Saint Nicholas, depicted him as a bishop complete with mitre and crook. The jolly old man dressed in red was a creation of 19th century America.

When Mohammed Ali was ruler of Egypt he created two infantry regiments consisting solely of one-eyed soldiers.

Table-tennis was first named 'gossamer'.

The amoeba consumes its food by wrapping its body round it.

Between 1812 and 1813 an American colonel, Russell Farnum, walked from St. Louis to Leningrad.

Otters cause no splash when they plunge into the water.

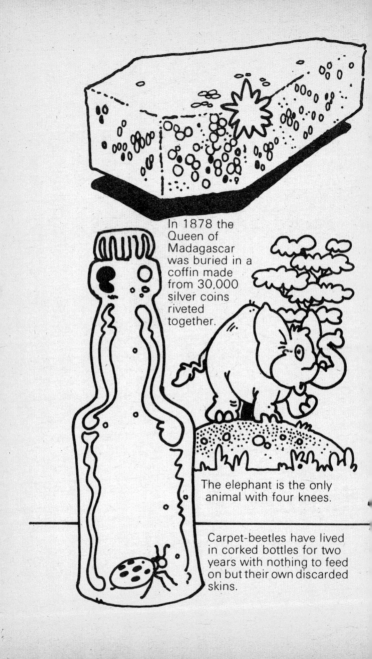

In 1878 the Queen of Madagascar was buried in a coffin made from 30,000 silver coins riveted together.

The elephant is the only animal with four knees.

Carpet-beetles have lived in corked bottles for two years with nothing to feed on but their own discarded skins.

The Basques are the only Christians to use the star of David on their grave stones.

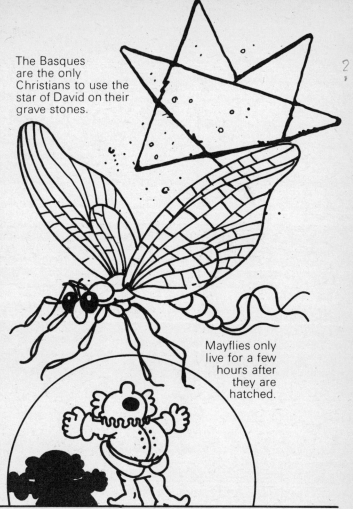

Mayflies only live for a few hours after they are hatched.

In 1831 the Italian operatic tenor Giovanni Rubini sang one high note with such force that he dislocated a collarbone.

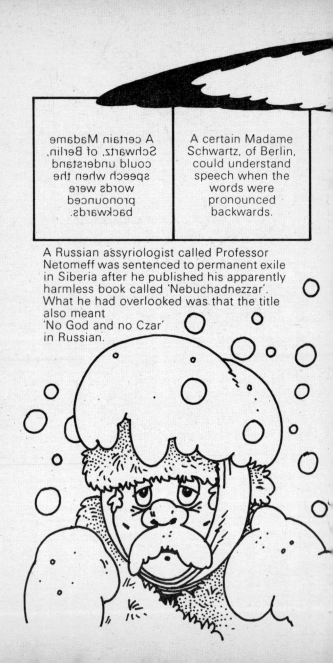

A certain Madame Schwartz, of Berlin, could understand speech when the words were pronounced backwards.

A certain Madame Schwartz, of Berlin, could understand speech when the words were pronounced backwards.

A Russian assyriologist called Professor Netomeff was sentenced to permanent exile in Siberia after he published his apparently harmless book called 'Nebuchadnezzar'. What he had overlooked was that the title also meant
'No God and no Czar'
in Russian.

An albatross can fly all day and not flap its wings once.

There is no soda in soda water.

Given that the average person uses a vocabulary of 3,000 words and speaks about 120 words a minute, he would be able to speak his total vocabulary in half an hour.

In Old English the daisy was called 'a daeges eage', 'the eye of the day', because it reminded people of the sun.

In 1660 a duty of four shillings (20 p) was levied on every gallon of coffee made and sold in England.

Surfing is one of the very few aquatic sports in which the participants wear bathing trunks, but try to keep out of the water.

A kiss has been medically described as 'the anatomical juxtaposition of two orbicularis oris muscles in a state of contraction.

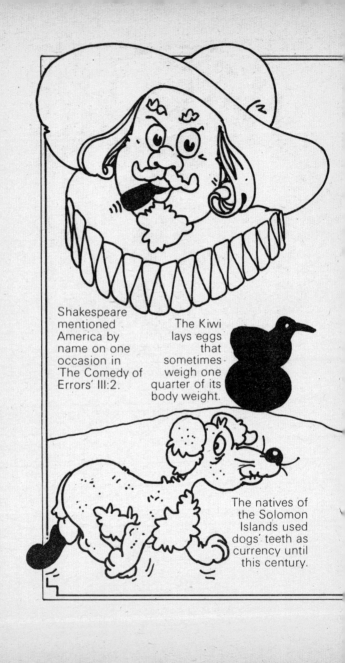

Shakespeare mentioned America by name on one occasion in 'The Comedy of Errors' III:2.

The Kiwi lays eggs that sometimes weigh one quarter of its body weight.

The natives of the Solomon Islands used dogs' teeth as currency until this century.

The luckiest number in Italy is 13.

A sixty-five-year-old man has about the same muscular power as a twenty-five-year-old woman.

The owl is the only bird capable of looking at an object with both eyes at the same time.

The flow of water in a channel on the Aegean island Euboea changes direction fourteen times every day.

'Biannual' means 'occurring twice a year'. 'Bimonthly' means 'occurring once every two months'.

Carlo Broschi
Farinelli, the
famous Italian
castrató of the
18th century,
was claimed to
be able to sing
seven or eight
notes above the
register of the
normal human
voice and to be
able to hold one
note for six
minutes.

The Holy Roman
Empire was
secular not holy,
it was German not
Roman, and the
Kings who ruled it
ruled in name
only, hardly mak-
ing it a complete
empire.

Francis of Lorraine, the son of Henry IV of France, was married when he was four years old. Even at that age he could be accused of being a cradle-snatcher since his wife was only three.

Marcus Licinius Crassus, who joined Caesar and Pompey in the first Roman triumvirate, made a fortune through the operation of a fire-fighting racket. By buying burning property at a fraction of its market value and then extinguishing the flames he acquired over £2,000,000 worth of property in Rome.

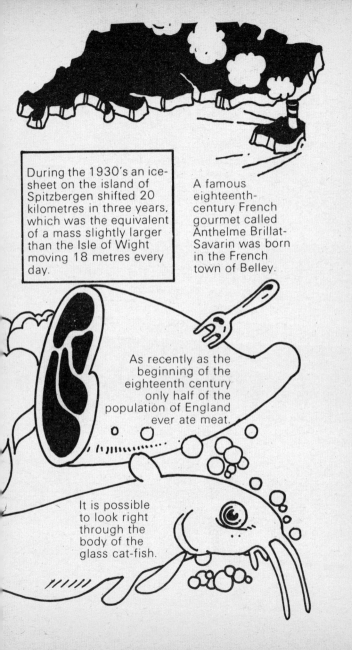

During the 1930's an ice-sheet on the island of Spitzbergen shifted 20 kilometres in three years, which was the equivalent of a mass slightly larger than the Isle of Wight moving 18 metres every day.

A famous eighteenth-century French gourmet called Anthelme Brillat-Savarin was born in the French town of Belley.

As recently as the beginning of the eighteenth century only half of the population of England ever ate meat.

It is possible to look right through the body of the glass cat-fish.

Some of the cells in our body are so small that 200,000 of them could fit onto the head of a pin.

In the two hundred and fifty years between 1564 and 1814 nine Frost Fairs were held on the Thames at Christmas time.

0.47 litres of petrol have the same explosive power as 0.45 kilogrammes of dynamite.

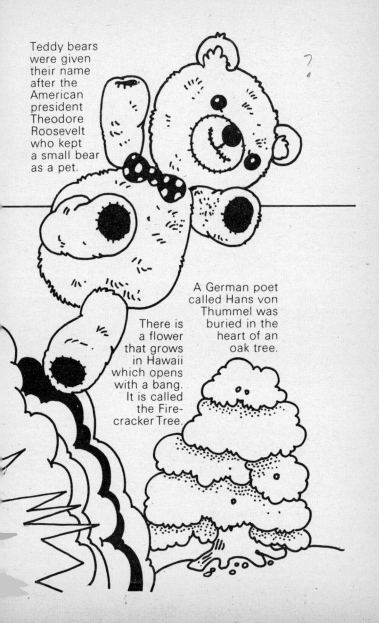

Teddy bears were given their name after the American president Theodore Roosevelt who kept a small bear as a pet.

A German poet called Hans von Thummel was buried in the heart of an oak tree.

There is a flower that grows in Hawaii which opens with a bang. It is called the Fire-cracker Tree.

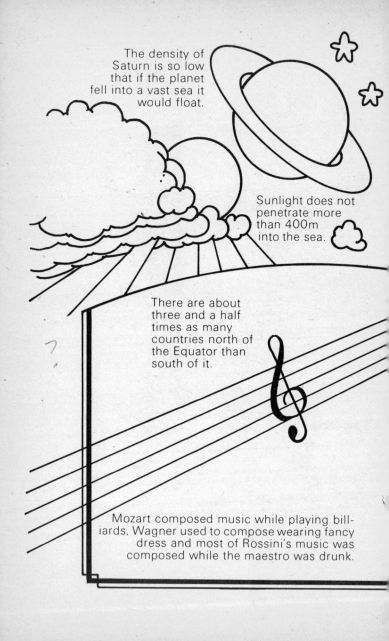

The density of Saturn is so low that if the planet fell into a vast sea it would float.

Sunlight does not penetrate more than 400m into the sea.

There are about three and a half times as many countries north of the Equator than south of it.

Mozart composed music while playing billiards, Wagner used to compose wearing fancy dress and most of Rossini's music was composed while the maestro was drunk.

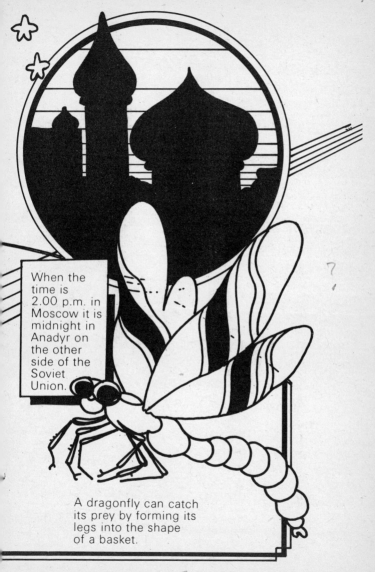

When the time is 2.00 p.m. in Moscow it is midnight in Anadyr on the other side of the Soviet Union.

A dragonfly can catch its prey by forming its legs into the shape of a basket.

The English expression 'forlorn hope' is derived from a Dutch expression meaning a 'lost troop', 'verloren hoop'.

In sixteenth-century Britain men were only allowed to beat their wives before 10.00 p.m.

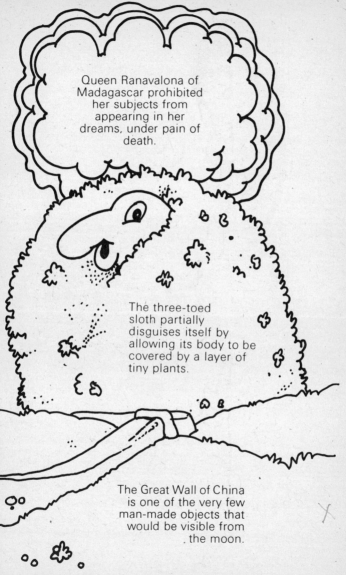

Queen Ranavalona of Madagascar prohibited her subjects from appearing in her dreams, under pain of death.

The three-toed sloth partially disguises itself by allowing its body to be covered by a layer of tiny plants.

The Great Wall of China is one of the very few man-made objects that would be visible from the moon.

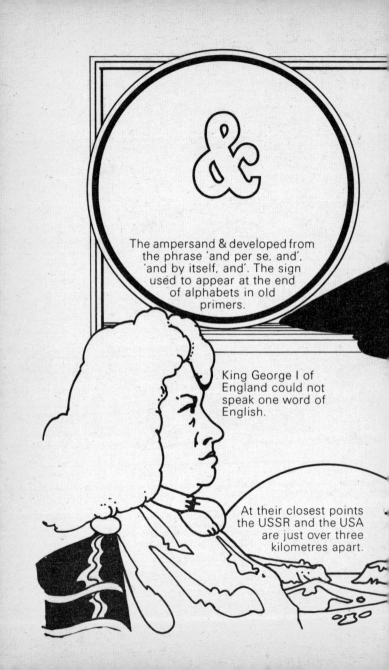

The ampersand & developed from
the phrase 'and per se, and',
'and by itself, and'. The sign
used to appear at the end
of alphabets in old
primers.

King George I of
England could not
speak one word of
English.

At their closest points
the USSR and the USA
are just over three
kilometres apart.

The great nineteenth-century actress Sarah Bernhardt played the part of Juliet at the age of seventy.

The American naval hero John Paul Jones ended his career commanding the Russian navy of Catherine the Great.

FICTION

GENERAL

☐ Stand on It	Stroker Ace	95p
☐ Chains	Justin Adams	£1.25
☐ The Master Mechanic	I. G. Broat	£1.50
☐ Wyndward Passion	Norman Daniels	£1.35
☐ Abingdon's	Michael French	£1.25
☐ The Moviola Man	Bill and Colleen Mahan	£1.25
☐ Running Scared	Gregory Mcdonald	85p
☐ Gossip	Marc Olden	£1.25
☐ The Sounds of Silence	Judith Richards	£1.00
☐ Summer Lightning	Judith Richards	£1.00
☐ The Hamptons	Charles Rigdon	£1.35
☐ The Affair of Nina B.	Simmel	95p
☐ The Berlin Connection	Simmel	£1.50
☐ The Cain Conspiracy	Simmel	£1.20
☐ Double Agent—Triple Cross	Simmel	£1.35
☐ Celestial Navigation	Anne Tyler	£1.00
☐ Earthly Possessions	Anne Tyler	95p
☐ Searching for Caleb	Anne Tyler	£1.00

WESTERN   BLADE SERIES

☐ No. 1	The Indian Incident	Matt Chisholm	75p
☐ No. 2	The Tucson Conspiracy	Matt Chisholm	75p
☐ No. 3	The Laredo Assignment	Matt Chisholm	75p
☐ No. 4	The Pecos Manhunt	Matt Chisholm	75p
☐ No. 5	The Colorado Virgins	Matt Chisholm	85p
☐ No. 6	The Mexican Proposition	Matt Chisholm	75p
☐ No. 7	The Arizona Climax	Matt Chisholm	85p
☐ No. 8	The Nevada Mustang	Matt Chisholm	85p

WAR

☐ Jenny's War	Jack Stoneley	£1.25
☐ The Killing-Ground	Elleston Trevor	£1.10

NAVAL HISTORICAL

☐ The Sea of the Dragon	R. T. Aundrews	95p
☐ Ty-Shan Bay	R. T. Aundrews	95p
☐ HMS Bounty	John Maxwell	£1.00
☐ The Baltic Convoy	Showell Styles	95p
☐ Mr. Fitton's Commission	Showell Styles	85p

FILM/TV TIE-IN

☐ American Gigolo	Timothy Harris	95p
☐ Meteor	E. H. North and F. Coen	95p
☐ Driver	Clyde B. Phillips	80p

SCIENCE FICTION

☐ The Mind Thing	Fredric Brown	90p
☐ Strangers	Gardner Dozois	95p
☐ Project Barrier	Daniel F. Galouye	80p
☐ Beyond the Barrier	Damon Knight	80p
☐ Clash by Night	Henry Kuttner	95p
☐ Fury	Henry Kuttner	80p
☐ Mutant	Henry Kuttner	90p
☐ Drinking Sapphire Wine	Tanith Lee	£1.25
☐ Journey	Marta Randall	£1.00
☐ The Lion Game	James H. Schmitz	70p
☐ The Seed of Earth	Robert Silverberg	80p
☐ The Silent Invaders	Robert Silverberg	80p
☐ City of the Sun	Brian M. Stableford	85p
☐ Critical Threshold	Brian M. Stableford	75p
☐ The Florians	Brian M. Stableford	80p
☐ Wildeblood's Empire	Brian M. Stableford	80p
☐ A Touch of Strange	Theodore Sturgeon	85p

NON-FICTION

GENERAL

☐ Guide to the Channel Islands — J. Anderson & E. Swinglehurst — 90p
☐ The Complete Traveller — Joan Bakewell — £1.95
☐ Time Out London Shopping Guide — Lindsey Bareham — £1.50
☐ World War 3 — Edited by Shelford Bidwell — £1.25
☐ The Black Angels — Rupert Butler — £1.35
☐ Hand of Steel — Rupert Butler — £1.35
☐ A Walk Around the Lakes — Hunter Davies — £1.50
☐ Truly Murderous — John Dunning — 95p
☐ In Praise of Younger Men — Sandy Fawkes — 85p
☐ Hitler's Secret Life — Glenn B. Infield — £1.50
☐ Wing Leader — Johnnie Johnson — £1.25
☐ Me, to Name but a Few — Spike Mullins — £1.00
☐ Our Future: Dr. Magnus Pyke Predicts — 95p
☐ The Devil's Bedside Book — Leonard Rossiter — 85p
☐ Barbara Windsor's Book of Boobs — Barbara Windsor — £1.50

BIOGRAPHY/AUTOBIOGRAPHY

☐ Go-Boy — Roger Caron — £1.25
☐ The Queen Mother Herself — Helen Cathcart — £1.25
☐ George Stephenson — Hunter Davies — £1.50
☐ The Queen's Children — Donald Edgar — £1.25
☐ Prince Regent — Harry Edgington — 95p
☐ All of Me — Rose Neighbour — £1.00
☐ Tell Me Who I Am Before I Die — C. Peters with T. Schwarz — £1.00
☐ Boney M — J. Shearlaw and D. Brown — 90p
☐ Kiss — John Swenson — 90p

HEALTH/SELF-HELP/POCKET HEALTH GUIDES

☐ Pulling Your Own Strings — Dr. Wayne W. Dyer — 95p
☐ The Pick of Woman's Own Diets — Jo Foley — 95p
☐ Woman X Two — Mary Kenny — 90p
☐ Cystitis: A Complete Self-help Guide — Angela Kilmartin — £1.00
☐ The Stress Factor — Donald Norfolk — 90p
☐ Fat is a Feminist Issue — Susie Orbach — 85p
☐ Related to Sex — Claire Rayner — £1.25
☐ The Working Woman's Body Book — L. Rowen with B. Winkler — 95p
☐ Woman's Own Birth Control — Dr. Michael Smith — £1.25
☐ Allergies — Robert Eagle — 65p
☐ Arthritis and Rheumatism — Dr. Luke Fernandes — 65p
☐ Back Pain — Dr. Paul Dudley — 65p
☐ Pre-Menstrual Tension — June Clark — 65p
☐ Migraine — Dr. Finlay Campbell — 65p
☐ Skin Troubles — Deanna Wilson — 65p

REFERENCE

☐ What's Wrong with your Pet? — Hugo Kerr — 95p
☐ You *Can* Train Your Cat — Jo and Paul Loeb — £1.50
☐ Caring for Cats and Kittens — John Montgomery — 95p
☐ The Oscar Movies from A-Z — Roy Pickard — £1.25
☐ Questions of Law — Bill Thomas — 95p
☐ The Hamlyn Book of Amazing Information — 80p
☐ The Hamlyn Family Medical Dictionary — £2.50

GAMES & PASTIMES

☐ The Hamlyn Book of Brainteasers and Mindbenders — Ben Hamilton — 85p
☐ The Hamlyn Book of Crosswords Books 1, 2, 3, and 4 — 60p
☐ The Hamlyn Book of Crosswords 5 — 70p
☐ The Hamlyn Book of Wordways 1 — 75p
☐ The Hamlyn Family Quiz Book — 85p

NON-FICTION

GENERAL COOKERY

KITCHEN LIBRARY SERIES

GARDENING/HOBBIES

NAME ....

ADDRESS ....

....

Write to Hamlyn Paperbacks Cash Sales, PO Box 11, Falmouth, Cornwall TR10 9EN.

Please indicate order and enclose remittance to the value of the cover price plus:

U.K.: 30p for the first book, 15p for the second book and 12p for each additional book ordered to a maximum charge of £1.29.

B.F.P.O. & EIRE: 30p for the first book, 15p for the second book plus 12p per copy for the next 7 books, thereafter 6p per book.

OVERSEAS: 50p for the first book plus 15p per copy for each additional book.

Whilst every effort is made to keep prices low it is sometimes necessary to increase cover prices and also postage and packing rates at short notice. Hamlyn Paperbacks reserve the right to show new retail prices on covers which may differ from those previously advertised in the text or elsewhere.